I0468211

Contents

About the Author

David Ye is a Chartered Financial Analyst (CFA) charter holder. He graduated with a Bachelor of Commerce degree majoring in Finance and Information Systems from the University of New South Wales Australia. In 2004, he received his CFA charter from the CFA Institute Virginia United States.

David has more than 15 years of investment experience across most asset classes. He has worked in insurance, banking, asset management and wealth management industries; servicing both institutional and private wealth clients.

In his free time, David enjoys Brazilian Jujitsu and yoga.

Email: simplified.fx.trading@gmail.com

Facebook: https://www.facebook.com/SimplifiedFXTrading

Preface

"The meaning of life is to find your gift. The purpose of life is to give it away." - Pablo Picasso

It was by coincidence that I started trading foreign exchange (FX) a couple of years ago. However, I have been investing in stocks and exchange traded funds (ETFs) since the dot com days back in 2000. There was an old saying that FX is a zero sum game and trading is the most difficult part of investing. It is a zero sum game because whenever there is a winner there would be a loser at the other end of the trade. For example with AUDUSD, the party who is long in AUD makes money when the other party who is short in AUD (long in USD) loses. The net economic gain is zero between the two parties.

I started trading FX with the intention to test out the option strategies I read from research reports and what I have learned during my academic studies. Strategies such as butterfly, straddle, and strangle etc. Names would appear to be confusing and meaningless to most of us. The results were mixed on per trade basis with a small overall positive returns. I thought to myself maybe it's time to develop my own strategies. In 2015, I simplified my trading strategies, improving and adapting them along the way. The performance has also improved and the portfolio returned +187.9% in 2015 (almost tripled in value) with a win percentage above 80% for all the trades done. All these were achieved by focusing on only one currency pair. For the same period, S&P 500 only returned +1.38%. The enclosed below is a return graph calculated by the broker on a time weighted basis for 2015.

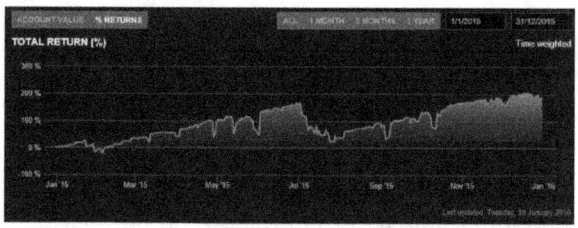

Source: Saxotrader

Performance was automatically calculated by Saxotrader (the broker) on their web portal. Past performance may not be repeated and is no guide for future performance. Past performance does not guarantee future results. As Saxotrader has not consented to the inclusion of the above graph for the general public, it is not liable for these statements under any applicable laws.

Introduction

Foreign exchange market is the largest and most liquid market in the world. Often it is this size and liquidity which draw investors and traders into it. However, it is also the most efficient market. This makes it the most difficult market to consistently outperform the peers. Very rarely you will find easy money in FX trades unless you are an intermediary which takes a huge spread (fees) for each transaction and then square off the position in the market immediately. Nevertheless, there are always hearsays about how people make money in FX consistently using fancy algorithm. There are a lot of FX books out there teaching people how to trade. Not many are written by actual traders who have an auditable winning track record. Most of them would prefer to keep their secrets and models private for obvious reasons.

Personally I have not read any FX trading books before I started trading. However I do have a good understanding of FX markets and investments from the Chartered Financial Analyst (CFA) Program I completed more than a decade ago coupled with investment experience across most asset classes since.

Some of the principles that I have learned and will share with you in this book may be transferrable to other asset classes such as equities and bonds. These include risk management and trading psychology. That being said, the trading strategies are only applicable to FX markets in most cases.

The purpose of this book is to share with you what has worked out well for me in term of FX trading. It is written in a reader's friendly fashion for both amateurs and professionals, and jargons free. It covers topics such as broker selection, risk budgeting, online resources, trading strategies, risk management, trading psychology and time management etc.

This book is not meant to serve as a bible or best practice guide. Rather it is a compilation of strategies and techniques which have worked out well for me. Needless to say there are a lot of successful FX traders out there who would consistently make bigger returns. However, they may not choose to share their secrets with the general public. I sincerely hope that this book would shed some lights on FX trading with you and hopefully you may walk away with something useful.

1. Getting Started

Trading is different from investing as it requires timely access to information and execution of trade ideas. Technologies can make this more efficient. There are three devices I use frequently to monitor the market and execute my trades during different times of the day.

Laptop

This should be the primary device to read daily news, doing analysis, formation of ideas and execution. You can do the same with a tablet. However, laptop is easier to use and has more functionalities. In term of software, you would need a web browser and Excel spreadsheet (you can get away with a calculator, however Excel is much faster and dynamic).

Tablet

A secondary device which can be used to read on breaking news and execute trades accordingly if necessary. It is smaller and easier to carry around. Make sure it has both cellular and wifi access.

Mobile Phone

Although most brokers allow you to execute trades via mobile phones nowadays, this is much more convenient to use tablet or laptop for execution because of more user friendly interface. However, phones are really useful for monitoring the prices since it is easier to be carried around.

Aside from these hardware, you are expected to have some basic understanding of economics and what factors may influence a currency. For example:

- Interest rate polices
- Inflation rate
- Unemployment rate
- GDP growth
- Housing Prices
- PMI (Purchasing Managers' Indices)

In addition, there are also some country (currency) specific data which you may need to know, depends on what currency pair you trade. For example, commodity prices and China data are important for AUD traders, and dairy product prices are important for NZD traders.

2. Broker Selection

This is perhaps one of the most important aspects of trading and it is also the least talked about. There are a few factors need to be considered before selecting a broker.

Online Access

The broker should offer you a stable online platform with minimum system outage for trading. The trading system should be user friendly and have some charting capability and provision of daily market news. In addition, a good broker would offer you online tracking of portfolio performance.

Size

The bigger the better. When you trade FX, the broker is the counterparty. Therefore, the bigger the counterparty the more liquidity they have and this would translate into better pricing. Furthermore, the bigger brokers are expected to have better coverage in term of different currency pairs and trade support in different time zone.

Spreads

A dollar saved is a dollar earned. Spread is the difference between bid and offer prices. You always buy at offer price and sell at a bid price. This means buy high and sell low. Every time you enter a trade you are already losing money even if the market doesn't move. This is because the spread the brokers take. Therefore a lower spread would help you to save money in long term. Spread varies between currency to currency, time of the day and the size of the trade. Major currencies are expected to have lower spread than minor currencies. Spread is lower during normal business hours than out of office hours. Therefore, it is important to choose a broker which has international operation and it covers different time zones. As for size of the trade, it can be a bit tricky. Spread can be low for small trade, however with big trade it can shoot up sometimes. This is because your counterparty want to protect themselves from sudden price jumps against them. Interestingly, if you trade at a high volume, spread is expected to go lower. However, you may need to pre-negotiate this with the broker. This works similarly to bulk buying discount.

What is a competitive spread? A competitive spread is around 1 to 2 pips (1 pip equals to 0.0001) for major currencies such as USD, EUR, JPY, GBP and AUD etc. It is expected to be higher for minor currencies.

Financial Strength

Whenever there is a currency crisis (a sudden and sharp drop in the value of a currency), there would be some brokers which are affected and forced to go bankrupt. If this happens, it could affect the money that you deposit in your trading account with the broker. The most recent event was the un-peg of Swiss Franc (CHF) in 2015. Therefore, it is important to choose a broker which is financially sound and have strong balance sheet. Ideally one which is affiliated with a bank. Banks are subject to under tighter regulations and closer supervisions in general.

Apart from the factors discussed above, there are also other factors that people may place emphasis on when engaging a broker. For example, research reports, seminars and innovative products offered.

Research Reports

Sometimes brokers like to differentiate themselves from the research reports and trade ideas they provide. Please bear in mind that most reports and ideas are generated by sell side analysts and their main objectives are to generate trade volumes. Sometimes they get it right and other times they may be wrong. The bottom line is that they create transactions and hence revenues for the firm. Buy side reports usually have more credibility as they tend to be more in-depth. The best research and trade ideas are the ones people actually put their own money into it. Unfortunately these are far and few out there for free. If you want to be a successful trader in the long run, it would be helpful if you start formulating your own trade ideas and learn from it rather than consistently relying on someone else's.

Seminars

Free seminars, it is often another sales pitch from brokers. In the world of trading and investment, there is no free meal. Free seminars are usually offered to people with a view to persuade them to sign up the relevant services and / or doing more trades after the seminars. It is good for beginners to participate such seminars to stay relevant and updated. However, you may not want to be overly excited with these seminars.

Innovative Products

Another sales gimmick which try to get you to either do more trades or/and charges a higher embedded fees from these innovative new products. The single most important factor when it comes to making money in FX is to get the direction right (whether you are long or short). The level of sophistication of the product only changes the embedded level of leverage (risk). If you get the direction right and use more leverage, you would make more money and vice versa. Leverage is like water, it can carry a ship and it can also sink a ship. Furthermore, leverage is not free and often it comes with a cost. The spot price of any currency pair is rather transparent and you can compare it easily between different brokers or simply looking at bid and offer spread. However, when it comes to innovative and broker specific products, it is extremely hard to compare the pricing competitiveness against its peers in the market. This enables the relevant stakeholders to make more fees / commissions on these premium products. Fees can be embedded in the pricing and often times they are not labelled as "fees". For example, change of implied volatilities and decay factor can affect the pricing of options. These conceptions are more for academic discussion which are beyond the scope of this book.

3. Source of Information

Trading focuses on short term price movement resulted from market volatilities. It is fundamentally different from investing. Hence, the information used to reach a trade decision can be different too. Old school investing is about fundamentals, valuations and growth potentials etc. This often requires reading and digesting a large chunk of information which covers an extensive period of time. Information required for trading is much simpler. Economic news for the day are usually the main drivers of the price volatilities. For example, it is not about reading the past 10 years economic data of a country before you decide if the currency is undervalued.

Most of the information required can be found from the following two websites and they are free.

Bloomberg

www.bloomberg.com

It provides updates of economic and market news and announcements.

Trading Economics
www.tradingeconomics.com

It provides a schedule of expected economic announcements for most countries.

These two web portals provide more than enough information to make daily trade decisions. The only additional piece of information is the charts of the currency pairs you are interested in trading. Most of the online brokers would provide this for free. You should try different brokers to find out which charting tools you are more comfortable with. Charts provide a guide of the price movement in the past and it is really a personal preference as to which type of charts to look at. Sometimes the simpler the better and in its rawest form rather than the fancy studies based on algorithm that some of the charting tools provide.

4. Risk Budget

Failure to plan is a plan to fail. Risk budget is a commonly used tool for institutional investors when they do their asset allocation and portfolio construction. However, it is probably the most neglected concept among retail investors. It dictates how much risk to take on and how much returns to expect accordingly. Investments are all about risk and returns. The same can be said for trading.

Below are a few simple steps which you can follow to derive your own risk budget

- What are your expected returns on a daily/monthly/yearly basis, whether it is in dollar amount or percentage.
- How much risk you are willing to take to generate these returns. Risk are measured in term of volatilities (deviation from the means). However, for the purpose of trading and simplicity we can use proxy instead of using spreadsheet to calculate precise historical volatilities of any underlying assets.

- The dollar amount required to achieve the expected returns given the predetermined level of risk.

For example, if you would like to generate $1000 profit a day with a capital of $250000, the expected daily returns would be 0.4%. If you are trading $250000 per ticket, the daily movement of the chosen currency is expected to be at least 0.4%. Of course, out of the $250000 capital, your equity could be much less with the use of leverage. Usually FX are traded on an initial margin basis, however you do need much more than the initial margin to implement good risk management techniques.

Now we know that we need a minimum of 0.4% movement on a daily basis (let's call it volatilities here for the purpose of discussion in this section although the real volatilities are calculated differently academically speaking). This would serve as a guide when we decide what currency pair to trade. If we choose a currency pair which has a lower volatilities, we would need to increase our capital / ticket size in order to achieve the expected returns. If we choose a currency pair which is more volatile, then a smaller ticket size would suffice. The currency pair we choose to trade would determine our implied level of volatilities or risk.

In short, the higher the expected risk the higher the expected returns would be. Risk can be controlled in two ways:

1. Volatility Of The Currency Pair

You can add on risk by choose a currency pair with higher volatilities and take away risk by trading a currency with lower volatilities.

2. Level Of Leverage In The Capital Structure

For the same currency pair you decide to trade, you can add on risk by having less equity and more debt (leverage) in your portfolio. When you put in more equity and reduce debt (leverage) in your portfolio you also reduce the level of risk.

Some people prefer lower underlying volatilities (of a currency pair) and enhanced with more leverage in the capital structure. Others would prefer more volatile currency with less leverage in the capital structure. It is this preference which would predetermine the currency pair to trade and focus in.

5. Selection of Trade Focus

Do not be a jack of all trades and master of none. When it comes to trading, it is better to be an expert in something rather than a generalist in everything.

Every day we are bombarded by information and market news about different countries and currencies. It seems there are opportunities everywhere. However, it is actually more productive and efficient to focus your trading on one pair of currency which you are most familiar with. There are only two scenarios for each currency pair, i.e. it either goes up or down. As long as you are on the right side you will make money. There is really no point having many different positions across different currency pairs. There is a huge monitoring cost for each currency pair you trade. Not only on the price movement, also the potential news flow and economic announcements which may affect the prices. If you are a trader who likes form your own trade decision rather than trade on grapevine, it is much better if you only focus on a particular pair of currency and all you have to decide is whether go long or short.

How to decide which currency pair to follow? There are a few factors to consider.

- Risk appetite

What kind of volatilities and expected returns are you looking for? Major currency pairs are less volatile than minor currency pairs in general. For example, if you are looking for high risk and high returns, then it would be minor or emerging market currencies. On the other hand, if you are looking for more stable currencies it would the G3 (USD, EUR and JPY).

- Familiarity with the countries and currencies

It is paramount that you choose a currency (country) that you understand. The good place to start with is the country of your residence and then pair it against the major currencies such as USD, EUR, GBP and JPY etc.

- Market Liquidity

Liquidity is an important factor to consider in order to keep the trading costs (bid and offer spread) low. Trading is a high volume game and you may want to minimize your transaction costs. A strong liquidity also prevents the possibility of price manipulations by large players.

- Access of Information

Information is power especially when it comes to trading. Choose a currency pair where information on both countries are easily available. This also ensures greater transparency and trading activities around the currency pair. This in turn would lead to better price efficiency and improved liquidity.

Lastly but not the least, it would be wise to avoid any controlled currency. Controlled currencies refer to currencies which have an artificial trading band imposed by central banks. As and when the central banks decide to lift the band, there would be huge price movement and a catalyst for margin calls and bankruptcy in the worst case scenario. The un-peg of CHF in 2015 is a very good example of this.

Once you decide on the pair of currency to trade, it is time to read as much as possible on news which may affect the movement of this currency pair and try to be an expert over time.

6. Trading Strategies

There are many roads lead to the top of the mountain. There are numerous strategies out there which have worked for different people over time. The strategies covered here are the ones which have been battle tested and performed well in 2015.

1. Trade When There Is No News

Most people like to trade when there are big announcements and hoping to be on the right side. The potential rewards can be huge and but so are the disappointments when you take the wrong side. Trading is different from investing. Trading is about taking small profits frequently and managing your losses accordingly; whereas investing is about letting your profit run and cut your losses early. Often time is the friend of investing, however it is the enemy of trading. This is because of the uncertainty and roll over costs. It is always better to be in cash and waiting for the next opportunities. This way you don't have to worry about market correction. That is why taking small profit often and stay in cash as much as you can. Cash is the king!

Market moves with or without news. The best time to trade is when the market moves in anticipation of something however there is no news announcement in the near horizon yet. For example, when a currency pair has moved for 0.5% for the day with no news, it is a good time to put in an initial opposite position. Please note this strategy only applies to FX trading and cannot be used for stock trading. Forex market is very liquid and efficient and it is less susceptible to manipulation and insider trading. However, equity market is different. There is always the risk of insider trading where people may have better information of the potential future price movement and try to establish positions before the actual news are announced. In addition, the frequency of news announcement are unpredictable for stocks. For example companies can issue profit warning at anytime, whilst the release schedule of economic news are always predetermined.

2. Be A Contrarian For The Day

It seems safe to be part of the herd. Often this is a false sense of security. This ties back to the previous point when there is no news and market is moving, it is the time to be a contrarian and take an opposite position. However, it is also important to recognise that the market can be persistent. Hence always be ready to average down your initial positions. For most major currency pairs, a 1% daily movement without any news announcement is considered significant. Most of them would just trade in the range until the announcement of the news.

The best position to be in is cash before any major announcement. After the news is announced and the market reacts, it is time to take the contrarian view and positioning for a quick rebound. The entry point for this strategy is the key. It is better to wait for the market to bottom out for the day before putting on the position rather than trying to catch a falling knife. One of the indicators is the double support level, i.e. the second time when the price touches the low during the day and bounces back.

3. Trade When Others Are Not Trading

Forex markets are dominated by institutional traders. These are the players which dictate the price movement and liquidity. Fortunately or unfortunately, corporate people tend to take lunch break which is usually between 12pm to 2pm. This is when the liquidity is thinner in the market and prices can move out of range. When this happens, it is a time to be a contrarian again. Market usually comes back down when the traders are back from lunch.

4. Dollar Cost Averaging

It is impossible to perfect the entry point of any trade. Sometimes you will find yourself entering a trade too early and market continues to fall. This is the time to use dollar cost averaging and lower your entry price. It is always prudent to have some cash for a few rounds of dollar cost averaging. The key is to start small and gradually increase your positions. Sometimes you may have to dollar cost average over a number of days. It is never wise to fight against the market, betting on a particular support level and go all in. Do remember that charts are only an indicator of what has happened in the past and future can be different. Most technical supports and ceilings would be broken in the long run.

5. Spot Versus Forward

Always start you trade with a spot contract as it is cheaper than forward. To trade a forward you would have to pay a premium for time value of money. The goal is to close your position before end of the trading day. However, if your position is losing money and you would like to average down your entry price level, it is a good time to consider weekly forward. The idea is when prices rebound (but not enough to bring in overall profit) you can choose to close your spot contracts first to avoid roll over costs and let the forward contract roll over until the next trading day. There is daily rolling cost for a spot contract, typically it is 2 to 3 pips (depends on the currency pair). If you end up rolling a spot contract for a week, it is actually cheaper to have a weekly forward contract in term of transaction costs. Remember when you are trading every pip counts.

6. Automated Trades And Price Triggers

Automated trades are the trades based on price triggers. It can be used for profit taking or cutting losses. Try to stay away from automated trades as they may bring in unnecessary losses when the market liquidity dries up during certain time of the day or week. For example, stop loss triggers may get activated when bid and offer widens by 100 pips and automated trades are triggered. Instead of using automated trades such as stop losses, it is more prudent to select the currency with appropriate volatility level and have enough cash reserves for margin calls.

7. Mean Reversion Happens

It is common for the prices to run up during beginning of the week under the influence of favourable news. By end of the week prices may come down slightly. This happens because traders would like to lock in their profits before the weekend to avoid uncertainty. Some countries like to release economic data and policy decisions over the weekend. When this happens, traders may get caught short without being able to offload their positions in time. The same anomaly may happen during end of the month too when traders like to lock in their profits to show a good scorecard to their bosses. These are all perfect opportunities for trading.

7. Risk Management - Margin of Safety

Do not put all your eggs in one basket. When it comes to investing in stocks, it is always about diversification. Currency trading is also about diversification. Rather than diversify into different currency pairs, it is more important to diversify the entry price point of the trade. Companies can go bankrupt and stock prices can go down to zero; hence there is a need to diversify your stock holdings into different companies. However, currencies do not go down to zero (although countries can go bankrupt too). A drop of 5% in a week is considered huge for any major currencies (provided they are not artificially pegged). Therefore, diversifying the entry point of the trade over time would help to lower the overall risk.

Another way to improve the margin of safety is to wait for initial price correction before initiating a trade. This would serve as a buffer. For example, if a currency has fallen for 1.5% intraday without any significant news, this would be a good entry point.

Always remember to have enough cash on the side to maintain margin of safety. Sometimes your brokers may increase the margin requirements for certain currency pairs during volatile market conditions. Without enough cash being set aside you may be forced to liquidate some of your positions and incur unnecessary trading costs and potential losses.

8. Risk Management - Taking Profits and Cutting Losses

When it comes to investing most people would tell you to let the profit run and cutting losses early. However, trading is the opposite. When it comes to trading you cannot be greedy. It is about taking small profits most of the time and managing your losses. A 0.5% gain is a decent profit level for a day trader for a major currency pair. A good loss cutting level is around 1% in most cases. The key is to improve your win percentage to 70% to 80%.

How to improve win percentage? Dollar cost average is the answer to that. That is why sometimes trading is a weighing game. A good weighing strategy can turn a losing position into a profitable one. Remember the margin of safety principle we discussed earlier, always to have cash to average down the entry price point.

9. Trading Psychology

Trading can be highly stressful sometimes especially when you are holding onto a losing position. This is when psychology comes into play. A good trader is the one who understand and control his/her emotions.

Greed and fear are the two constant companions. It is not about being greedy when others are fearful and fearful when others are greedy. Rather it is about being content when greed speaks to you. Taking a small profit and closing the day with all cash position is always better than leaving your position overnight and hoping for more gains tomorrow. The opposite can often happen and wipe out all your gains. When fear comes in, it is time to assess the situation and start to average down your position and looking for better exit point on the rebound. No one cashes out at the peak consistently, but you also do not want to be the one who exits when it is bottoming out.

When you are confused and not sure what to do, ask yourself this question. Are you losing sleep over the open position? If you are, it is time to close it and fight another day. Do not hold onto a losing position and hope for the best. No one can have 100% win ratio, it is how you deal with the losses that makes you a good trader.

Remember trading is a marathon, not a sprint. Slow and steady profits will bring you there eventually.

10. The Ten Commandments of Trading

1.   Risk Only What You Can Afford To Lose
Trading is a risky and it usually involves leverage. Only risk what you can afford to lose. Never put your lifestyle on the line.

2.   Trade What You Understand
Both markets and financial instruments are complex in nature. Trading is very competitive. It is better to be a specialist and trade selectively than to follow the crowd and trade everything under the sun.

3.   Liquidity And Transparency Are Important
Choose a currency pair which is liquid and transparent. Never trade a currency pair which is artificially controlled by the government or central banks.

4.   It Is Only A Profit When You Close The
      Position
Unrealised profit is not real and unfortunately unrealised losses are. It is always a good idea to take a small profit, raise cash and live to trade another day.

5.   No One Has 100% Win Percentage

No one is right all the time. Period. Deal with your losses and don't let them balloon out. You have to learn to take losses to survive in this game. Sometimes it is a good idea to take small losses in order to avoid even bigger ones.

6.   Taking No Position Is Also A Position

It is ok to sitting on cash and do nothing. Cash is the king. You have to be patient to make money. That includes waiting for the right trading opportunity.

7.   Margin Of Safety And Dollar Cost Average Are Your Friends

Margin of Safety would help you to improve your win percentage and dollar cost average can save you from a losing position.

8.   Leverage Is Like Water Use Wisely

Leverage is like water, it can float the ship and also sink the ship. When you are on the right side of the trade it magnifies the profit, and unfortunately if you are on the wrong side it can really hurt you with big losses. When greed speaks to you, be content. When caution speaks to you, listen and deleverage.

9. Nothing Beats A Good Night Sleep
Both market and trading are uncertain and anything can happen. If you are losing sleep about a position, close it. Listen to your gut feelings.

10. Trading Is A Marathon Not A Sprint
Trading is about taking small profits consistently and avoiding big losses. Do not be greedy and hope to hit it big overnight. Enjoy the journey and learn along the way. You will be rewarded as time goes on.

11. Time Management

Time is a finite resource for everyone and it does not discriminate. As a retail trader you are competing against the big boys (institutional players) in the market where they would have more resources both technological and human. It is important to level the play field by allocate your time wisely.

Often the less is more. Instead of focusing on everything going on in the market, it is more beneficial to drill down on the news which affect the currency pair you are trading. You do not need to trade all the currency pairs to make money, one currency pair is enough if you can be on the right side. Be selective and a specialist in one pair and over time you will see the rewards. Every day you will hear stories that people make big monies from trading a particular pair of currency, do not go and chase the wild goose, stay and focus on the one pair that you trade.

Forex market opens almost 24 hours a day and 5 days a week. However, it does not mean you have to be trading whenever the market is open. Good time management skills would bring longevity into trading. It is always good by starting the day to catch up on the market news and wait for market to establish its rhythm of the day before initiating the position.

Once the initial position is open, you should walk away from the computer and get on with your daily routines. It is only necessary to check the price level every 2 to 3 hours until the position is closed during the day. Before you go to bed, it is the time to decide whether to leave it open or close for the day. It is always better to have all in cash and not to worry about anything when you are sleeping. A small profit is better than no profit and a small loss is definitely better than a big loss.

12. A Balanced Lifestyle

Trading can be fun and rewarding. However, it is not an easy job. It is never about sitting by the pool and making money by just clicking your mouse button. Well, that may be the end product but there are a lot of planning, strategising, discipline and emotional roller coasters involved.

It is also highly demanding both physically and mentally if you want to stay on top of your game day in and day out. It is more like a sports where you need to lead a healthy lifestyle to stay competitive. It is about getting enough sleep, eating right, working out and be disciplined with your training/trading routines.

A typical trading day would be like getting up early and reading through the market news and forthcoming announcements of the day. Strategising and planning for your positions, and wait for the market to present the opportunities to you. Once the position is open, it would then require periodic monitoring. You do not have to glue yourself to the screen. Before you go to bed, you would have to make a major decision whether to leave the positions open or cash out and be worry free.

However, trading should not be everything you do in a day. It is important to spend time to do the things you enjoy rather than gluing yourself to the monitor and thinking about the open position all the time. To be a good trader you need to have mental clarity and stay sharp all the time. The only way to achieve that is to have a balanced lifestyle, taking time out to do things which you truly enjoy and takes your mind away from the market. It can be running, yoga, swimming, martial arts or any kind of hobby which refreshes your mind.

Furthermore, it is also beneficial to take a vacation every now and then, and be completely away from the market and recharge your batteries. Never go on a holiday with any open position. It would keep your mind preoccupied and you may not be able to enjoy the holiday at all.

Lastly, luck also plays a part when it comes to trading. So good karma is important. Pay it forward when the market rewards you and share the joy with others.

Conclusion

Trading is different from investing. Trading focuses on small price movements resulting from the imbalances in the liquidity in the market whilst investing is about discovering undervalued assets and holding them for long term. Trading is about taking small profits frequently and at the same time managing losses. It is important to improve the win ratio in order to be profitable in the long term. Margin of safety and dollar cost average are great ways to improve the win percentage.

It pays to be a specialist in one or two currency pairs rather than a generalist and trading everything. It is important to select the right broker and keep the trading costs low.

Trading can be both physically and mentally demanding, therefore it is important to live a balanced lifestyle. You need to look after your body and spending time doing the things you enjoy. Do not burn yourself out from trading. It is a marathon rather than a sprint. Take your time and enjoy the journey.

Disclaimer

This book is for general information only. No information, forward looking statements, or estimations presented herein represent any final determination on investment performance. While the information presented in this book has been researched and is thought to be reasonable and accurate, any trading or investment is speculative in nature. The author cannot and do not guarantee any rate of return based on the information presented herein.

By reading and reviewing the information contained in this book, the reader acknowledges and agrees that the author does not assume and hereby disclaim any liability to any party for any loss or damage caused by the use of the information contained herein, or errors or omissions in the information contained in this book, to make any trading or investment decision, whether such errors or omissions result from negligence, accident or any other cause.

Readers are required to conduct their own investigations, analysis, due diligence, draw their own conclusions, and make their own decisions. Any areas concerning taxes or specific legal or technical questions should be referred to lawyers, accountants, consultants, brokers, or other professionals licensed, qualified or authorized to render such advice.

In no event shall the author be liable to any party for any direct, indirect, special, incidental, or consequential damages of any kind whatsoever arising out of the use of this book or any information contained herein. The author specifically disclaim any guarantees, including, but not limited to, stated or implied potential profits, rates of return, or investment timelines.

Past performance may not be repeated and is no guide for future performance. Past performance does not guarantee future results.